CAROLS FOR CHRISTMAS

Compiled and arranged by DAVID WILLCOCKS

THE METROPOLITAN MUSEUM OF ART and
HOLT, RINEHART AND WINSTON, New York

I am grateful for the valuable assistance of

Julian Shuckburgh

in the preparation of this volume.

For acknowledgments, see page 92.

Published by The Metropolitan Museum of Art, New York, and
Holt, Rinehart and Winston,
383 Madison Avenue, New York, New York 10017

Produced by the Department of Special Publications,
The Metropolitan Museum of Art
Designed by Peter Oldenburg
Music engraved by Chapman Associates, Burlington, Vermont
Printed and bound by A. Mondadori, Verona, Italy

LIBRARY OF CONGRESS CATALOGING IN PUBLICATION DATA
Main entry under title:

Carols for Christmas.

   "Each of the hymns and carols in this book can be sung unaccompanied
by four or more voices, or sung by solo voice with piano, or played on the
piano alone"—
Introd.
   1. Carols, English. 2. Hymns, English. 3. Christmas music.
I. Willcocks, David, 1919–

M2065.C26   1983   83-8596

ISBN 0-87099-345-3
ISBN 0-03-064044-X (Holt, Rinehart and Winston)

10 9 8 7 6 5 4 3 2

ISBN 0-03-064044-X

TABLE OF CONTENTS

This book is for
those who love music and the visual arts.

INTRODUCTION

IT IS REMARKABLE that carol singing, the gathering of singers around the fireside or in the streets at Christmas time, should still prosper in our own age. This innocent and delightful ritual survives in our secular society, despite the commercialization of Christmas and the age of television and mass entertainment. It has outlasted many other customs that have disappeared in the face of modern pressures, and other rites that had a less certain hold on people's true feelings. It still symbolizes to us the spirit of peace and brotherhood, the unity of the family, and the values of stable community life—ideals that transcend its Christian meaning.

The carols and Christmas hymns contained in this book have become popular over the years and have stood the test of time. Some of them appear here in their original form, others have been specially arranged. In making the arrangements my aim has been simplicity, since there are already in existence some good carol books containing more elaborate settings suitable for choirs, with or without organ or orchestral accompaniment. Each of the hymns and carols in this book can be sung unaccompanied by four or more voices, or sung by solo voice with piano, or played on the piano alone.

Apart from the pleasures of communal singing, much of the appeal of carols lies in the simplicity of their musical form. In its earliest usage the word *carol* seems to have been synonymous with dance as well as song, and the lilt of the dance measure can be felt in most of the early melodies (note how many of the carols in this book are in three-eight or six-eight time). The medieval ring dance known as the *carole* comprised a simple form, the alternation between verse and refrain, a solo singer and dancer alternating with the group. The Church in the Middle Ages succeeded in suppressing the dance element, although this element had evidently been an integral part of religious worship in many societies from earliest times. (Instances of it abound in the Old Testament, for example, as in the precept in Psalm 149: "Let the children of Zion be joyful in their King. Let them praise his name in the dance.") The carol also has clear affinities with other forms of folk song, such as the ballad with its repeated four-line melody. Such simple popular forms have stayed in the mainstream of the carol tradition and have rarely been departed from even by carol composers of the last hundred years.

The words of many of our most familiar carols have links with pre-Christian cults like the Roman Saturnalia or the pagan yule festival. The burning of the yule log, the boar's head, the display of evergreen holly-and-ivy decorations are all ancient symbols of regeneration, fertility, and rebirth, and in the course of time it was natural that they should become associated with the great Christian feast of Christmas. The words of many other carols have medieval roots, and are redolent of the spontaneity and simplicity of rural life and full of that imagery of the nativity that is also to be found in the great English mystery and miracle plays.

We owe much of the medieval spirit of Christmas that survives today to the Franciscans. Saint Francis of Assisi himself is said to have made the first crèche at Greccio in 1223, three years before his death, but the custom of setting up crèches may date back even earlier. Within a hundred years the tradition had spread throughout Europe and become more elaborate, with priests, monks, and children acting the parts of shepherds and angels. The miracle plays, such as those of York, Chester, and Coventry, soon followed, and they in turn were a great stimulus to the writing of Christmas songs. (A late eighteenth-century crèche can be seen on page 88 of this book, where elaborately painted and richly clad Neapolitan figures decorate The Metropolitan Museum of Art Christmas tree.)

After the Protestant Reformation carolers had a lean time, but there was a revival of interest in carol singing in the eighteenth century, when old carols began to be rediscovered and new ones composed. In the nineteenth century these twin processes gathered pace, and it is to this period that we owe some of the most beautiful and beloved of all carols, such as "Once in Royal David's City," "Away in a Manger," and "We Three Kings of Orient Are."

A rich source of Christmas music has been the French carol tradition, based on the *noël*. The *noël* developed late in the fifteenth century, at a time when the carol was well established in England. Unlike English carols, however, it was exclusively connected with Christmas. It is distinguished by no particular metrical form, although dance tunes are common. There are seven carols of French origin in this collection, ranging in date from the fifteenth century (the tune of "O Come, O Come, Emmanuel") to the eighteenth ("Patapan," composed by Bernard de la Monnoye [1641–1728], first published in 1842).

The carols and hymns in this collection stem from diverse sources and are drawn from many parts of the world, including—besides England and the United States—Czechoslovakia, France, Germany, Poland, and Wales. In some instances, such as "In the Bleak Midwinter" (words by Christina Rossetti/music by Gustav Holst) and "Once in Royal David's City" (C. F. Alexander/H. J. Gauntlett), the name of both author and composer is known; in some, such as "Away in a Manger" (tune by W. J. Kirkpatrick) and "O Little One Sweet" (tune by J. S. Bach), the identity of the composer is known but not that of the author. In some carols, such as "Good Christian Men, Rejoice" (words by J. M. Neale) and "Ding Dong! Merrily on High" (words by G. R. Woodward), the identity of the author is known but not that of the composer.

The words of certain carols are original; the words of others are a translation, ranging from the literal, as in "O Come, All Ye Faithful" (translated from Latin by F. Oakeley and W. T. Brooke) to the free, as in "Lo, How a Rose" (translated from German). This latter carol indeed spans the centuries, since the seventh-century words, translated in the nineteenth century, are wedded to an ancient melody harmonized in the early seventeenth century by Michael Praetorius.

In most carols the music is original, while in a few it is adapted. In "Joy to the World!," for example, Lowell Mason has adapted part of a chorus by George Frederick Handel, and in "Hark! The Herald Angels Sing," W. H. Cummings has adapted a chorus by Mendelssohn (under whom Cummings sang as a choirboy) and compiled the verbal text from three sources (C. Wesley for verse 1, G. Whitefield for verse 2, and M. Madan for verse 3).

About a dozen of the carols are classed as "English traditional," their authorship unknown and their words and tunes handed down from generation to generation. Some are associated with a particular region of England—the "Sussex Carol" ("On Christmas night all Christians sing") with Sussex, "Wassail, Wassail" with Gloucestershire, the "Sans Day Carol" ("Now the holly bears a berry") with Cornwall—while others have been used more widely, resulting in many local variants of both words and music. That there is such a rich store of traditional English carols available to us today is due in no small part to the painstaking research of certain Victorian scholars—William Sandys, H. R. Bramley, and John Stainer, for example—who published collections of carols. Their important work in this field was continued into the twentieth century by Cecil Sharp, to whom we owe "The Holly and the Ivy," and by Ralph Vaughan Williams, who notated and arranged the "Sussex Carol."

By the nineteenth century the English-speaking world across the Atlantic was beginning to make its own contributions to the Christmas carol. Because the men and women who left seventeenth-century England for the New World were usually dissenters, they rarely took with them anything to remind them of the great medieval tradition in Church music. We must be grateful to their tradition as it developed in its own soil for some beautiful carols, including "Away in a Manger" and "We Three Kings of Orient Are."

Within their simple forms, carols display a wide variety of rhythm and melodic line as well as verbal imagery. The delight in carol singing has much to do with the changes in mood between, for example, the exuberance of "We Wish You a Merry Christmas" and the gentle lullaby of "Rocking," or the ancient plain-chant-like melody of "Lo, How a Rose" and the romantic effect of Peter Cornelius's tune above the old German chorale "Wie schön leuchtet," as harmonized by Sir Ivor Atkins in "The Three Kings." These changes in mood are dramatic, but always are achieved by simple musical means. Carol music is essentially simple—the ancient, unalterable music of the people. Perhaps that is why it lives on.

Alongside the carols in this collection are reproductions of great paintings, sculpture, and prints, spanning the centuries, from the fine collections of The Metropolitan Museum of Art in New York. It is my hope that this book will be especially welcome in the homes of those who enjoy music and appreciate art.

DAVID WILLCOCKS

HARK! THE HERALD ANGELS SING

Words by Charles Wesley, George Whitefield, and **Martin Madan** (slightly adapted)

Tune by Felix Mendelssohn (slightly adapted)

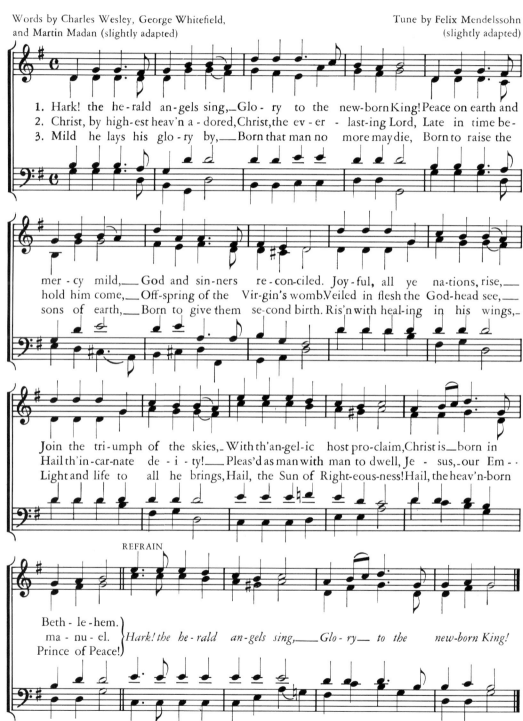

1. Hark! the he-rald an-gels sing,—Glo-ry to the new-born King! Peace on earth and
2. Christ, by high-est heav'n a - dored, Christ, the ev - er - last-ing Lord, Late in time be-
3. Mild he lays his glo-ry by,—Born that man no more may die, Born to raise the

mer - cy mild,—God and sin-ners re-con-ciled. Joy-ful, all ye na-tions, rise,—
hold him come,—Off-spring of the Vir-gin's womb Veiled in flesh the God-head see,—
sons of earth,—Born to give them se-cond birth. Ris'n with heal-ing in his wings,—

Join the tri-umph of the skies,—With th'an-gel-ic host pro-claim, Christ is—born in
Hail th'in-car-nate de - i - ty!—Pleas'd as man with man to dwell, Je - sus,—our Em —
Light and life to all he brings, Hail, the Sun of Right-eous-ness! Hail, the heav'n-born

REFRAIN

Beth - le - hem.
ma - nu - el.   Hark! the he - rald an-gels sing,—Glo-ry— to the new-born King!
Prince of Peace!

O LITTLE TOWN OF BETHLEHEM

Words by Phillips Brooks

Tune by Lewis H. Redner

1. O lit - tle town of Beth - le - hem, How still we see thee lie!
2. For Christ is born of Ma - ry, And ga - ther'd all a - bove,

A - bove thy deep and dream - less sleep The si - lent stars go by.
While mor - tals sleep, the an - gels keep Their watch of won - d'ring love.

Yet in thy dark streets shin - eth The ev - er - last - ing light;
O morn - ing stars, to - ge - ther Pro - claim the ho - ly birth,

The hopes and fears of all the years Are met in thee to - night.
And prais - es sing to God the King, And peace to men on earth.

3. How silently, how silently,
   The wondrous gift is giv'n!
   So God imparts to human hearts
   The blessings of his heav'n.
   No ear may hear his coming;
   But in this world of sin,
   Where meek souls will receive him, still
   The dear Christ enters in.

4. O holy child of Bethlehem,
   Descend to us, we pray;
   Cast out our sin and enter in,
   Be born in us today.
   We hear the Christmas angels
   The great glad tidings tell:
   O come to us, abide with us,
   Our Lord Emmanuel.

IT CAME UPON THE MIDNIGHT CLEAR

Words by Edmund H. Sears

Tune by Richard S. Willis

1. It came up - on___ the mid - night clear, That glo - rious song_of old, From an - gels bend - ing near the earth To touch their harps_of gold: "Peace on the earth___ good - will___ to men From heav'n's_all - gra - cious King!" The world__ in sol - emn still - ness lay___ To hear the an - gels sing.

2. Still through the clo - ven skies they come, With peace-ful wings_un - furled; And still their heav'n-ly mu - sic floats O'er all the wea - ry world; A - bove its sad___ and low - ly plains They bend___ on ho - v'ring wing; And ev - er o'er___ its Ba - bel sounds_ The bless - ed an - gels sing.

3. Yet with the woes of sin and strife
   The world has suffered long;
   Beneath the angel strain have rolled
   Two thousand years of wrong;
   And man, at war with man, hears not
   The love song which they bring:
   O hush the noise, ye men of strife,
   And hear the angels sing!

4. For lo! the days are hast'ning on,
   By prophet-bards foretold,
   When, with the ever-circling years,
   Comes round the age of gold;
   When peace shall over all the earth
   Its ancient splendors fling,
   And the whole world send back the song
   Which now the angels sing.

GOOD CHRISTIAN MEN, REJOICE

Words by John Mason Neale

German traditional carol

1. Good Chris-tian men,— re-joice———— With heart, and soul,— and voice;————
2. Good Chris-tian men,— re-joice———— With heart, and soul,— and voice;————
3. Good Chris-tian men,— re-joice———— With heart, and soul,— and voice;————

Give ye heed to what we say: Je-sus Christ is born to-day.
Now ye hear of end-less bliss: Je-sus Christ was born for this!
Now ye need not fear the grave: Je-sus Christ was born to save!

Ox and ass be-fore him bow, And he is in—— the man-ger now.
He has ope'd the heav'n-ly door, And man is bless-ed ev-er-more.
Calls you one and calls you all, To gain his ev-er-last-ing hall.

Christ is born to-day!———— Christ is born to-day!
Christ was born for this!———— Christ was born for this!
Christ was born to save!———— Christ was born to save!

ANGELS WE HAVE HEARD

Words traditional

Old French tune

1. An - gels we have heard on high, Sweet-ly sing-ing o'er__ the plains. And the moun-tains in re - ply, E - cho-ing__ their__ joy-ous strain.
2. Shep-herds why this ju - bi - lee? Why your joy-ous__ strains pro - long? What the glad-some ti - dings be, Which in - spire__ your__ heav'n-ly song?

REFRAIN

Glo - - - - - - - - - - - - - - ri - a in__ ex - cel - sis De - o.__

Glo - - - - - - - - - - - - - - ri - a in__ ex - cel - sis De - o.

ON HIGH

3. Come to Bethlehem and see
   Him whose birth the
      angels sing;
   Come, adore on bended knee
   Christ, the Lord, the newborn
      King.
   Gloria in excelsis Deo, etc.

4. See him in a manger laid,
   Whom the choirs of
      angels praise;
   Mary, Joseph, lend your aid,
   While our hearts in love
      we raise.
   Gloria in excelsis Deo, etc.

AWAY IN A MANGER

Words anonymous

Tune by William James Kirkpatrick

1. A - way in a__ man-ger, No__ crib for a bed,
2. The cat - tle are__ low-ing, The__ ba - by a - wakes,
3. Be near me, Lord Je - sus; I__ ask thee to stay

The__ lit - tle Lord Je - sus Laid__ down his sweet head.
But__ lit - tle Lord Je - sus No__ cry - ing he makes.
Close__ by me for - ev - er, And__ love me, I pray.

The stars in the__ bright sky Look'd down where he lay,
I love thee, Lord__ Je - sus! Look__ down from the sky,
Bless all the dear__ chil - dren In__ thy ten - der care,

The__ lit - tle Lord Je - sus A - sleep__ on__ the__ hay.
And__ stay by my cra - dle Till__ morn-ing is__ nigh.
And__ fit us for hea - ven, To__ live__ with__ thee__ there.

21

GOOD KING WENCESLAS

Words by John Mason Neale

Tune from *Piae Cantiones*, 1582

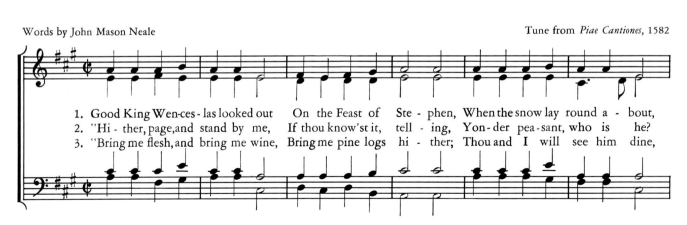

1. Good King Wen-ces-las looked out   On the Feast of   Ste-phen, When the snow lay round a-bout,
2. "Hi-ther, page, and stand by me,   If thou know'st it,   tell-ing, Yon-der pea-sant, who is   he?
3. "Bring me flesh, and bring me wine,   Bring me pine logs   hi-ther; Thou and I will   see him   dine,

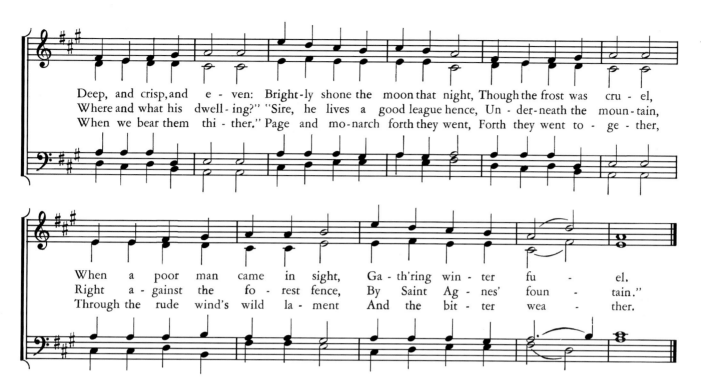

Deep, and crisp, and e - ven: Bright-ly shone the moon that night, Though the frost was cru - el,
Where and what his dwell-ing?" "Sire, he lives a good league hence, Un - der-neath the moun-tain,
When we bear them thi - ther." Page and mo-narch forth they went, Forth they went to - ge - ther,

When a poor man came in sight, Ga - th'ring win - ter fu - el.
Right a - gainst the fo - rest fence, By Saint Ag - nes' foun - tain."
Through the rude wind's wild la - ment And the bit - ter wea - ther.

4. "Sire, the night is darker now,
   And the wind blows stronger;
   Fails my heart, I know not how,
   I can go no longer."
   "Mark my footsteps, good my page!
   Tread thou in them boldly:
   Thou shalt find the winter's rage
   Freeze thy blood less coldly."

5. In his master's steps he trod,
   Where the snow lay dinted;
   Heat was in the very sod
   Which the saint had printed.
   Therefore, Christian men, be sure,
   Wealth or rank possessing,
   Ye who now will bless the poor,
   Shall yourselves find blessing.

If this carol is sung in unison with accompaniment,
the following arrangement is suggested:

Verse 1: all singers
Verse 2, lines 1 – 4: men only; lines 5 – 8: women or boys
Verse 3, lines 1 – 4: men only; lines 5 – 8: all singers
Verse 4, lines 1 – 4: women or boys; lines 5 – 8: men only
Verse 5: all singers

THE FIRST NOWELL

English traditional carol

1. The first Nowell the angel did say, Was to certain poor shepherds in fields as they lay; In
2. They looked up and saw a star, Shining in the east, beyond them far; And
3. And by the light of that same star, Three wise men came from country far; To

fields where they lay keeping their sheep, On a cold winter's night that was so deep.
to the earth it gave great light, And so it continued both day and night.
seek for a king was their intent, And to follow the star wherever it went.

REFRAIN

Nowell, Nowell, Nowell, Nowell, Born is the King of Israel.

4. This star drew nigh to the northwest,
O'er Bethlehem it took its rest,
And there it did both stop and stay
Right over the place where Jesus lay.
Nowell, Nowell, etc.

5. Then entered in those wise men three,
Full rev'rently upon their knee,
And offer'd there, in his presence,
Their gold, and myrrh, and frankincense.
Nowell, Nowell, etc.

6. Then let us all with one accord
Sing praises to our heav'nly Lord,
That hath made heav'n and earth of nought,
And with his blood mankind hath bought.
Nowell, Nowell, etc.

O LITTLE ONE SWEET

Translated by Percy Dearmer

Tune by Johann Sebastian Bach

1. O little one sweet, O little one mild, Thy Father's purpose thou hast fulfilled; Thou cam'st from heav'n to mortal ken, Equal to be with us poor men, O little one sweet, O little one mild.

2. O little one sweet, O little one mild, With joy thou hast the whole world filled; Thou camest here from heav'n's domain, To bring men comfort in their pain, O little one sweet, O little one mild.

3. O little one sweet, O little one mild,
In thee love's beauties are all distilled;
  Then light in us thy love's bright flame,
  That we may give thee back the same,
O little one sweet, O little one mild.

4. O little one sweet, O little one mild,
Help us to do as thou hast willed.
  Lo, all we have belongs to thee!
  Ah, keep us in our fealty!
O little one sweet, O little one mild.

BRING A TORCH, JEANNETTE, ISABELLA

Translated by E. Cuthbert Nunn

French traditional carol

1. Bring a torch, Jean-nette, Is - a - bel - la! Bring a torch, to the cra - dle run!
2. It is wrong when the child is sleep - ing, It is wrong to talk so loud;
3. Soft - ly to the lit - tle sta - ble, Soft - ly for a mo - ment come;

It is Je - sus, good folk of the vil - lage; Christ is born and Ma - ry's call - ing.
Si - lence, all, as you ga - ther a - round, Lest your noise should wa - ken Je - sus.
Look and see how charm - ing is Je - sus, How he is warm, his cheeks are ro - sy.

Ah! ah! beau - ti - ful is the mo - ther!
Hush! hush! see how fast he slum - bers;
Hush! hush! see how the child is sleep - ing;

Ah! ah! beau - ti - ful is her son!
Hush! hush! see how fast he sleeps!
Hush! hush! see how he smiles in dreams.

29

BOAR'S HEAD CAROL

English traditional carol

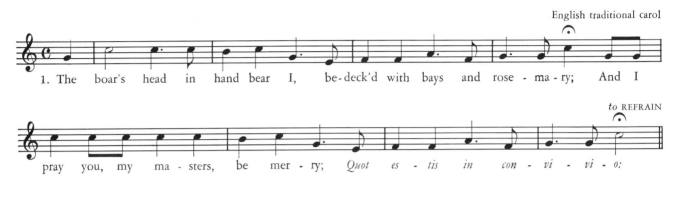

1. The boar's head in hand bear I, be-deck'd with bays and rose-ma-ry; And I
pray you, my ma-sters, be mer-ry; *Quot es-tis in con-vi-vi-o:*

to REFRAIN

2. The boar's head, as I un-der-stand, Is the rar-est dish in all this land, Which
thus be-deck'd with a gay gar-land, Let us *ser-vi-re can-ti-co:*

to REFRAIN

3. Our stew-ard hath pro-vid-ed thus, In ho-nor of the King of bliss, Which

to REFRAIN

on this day to be serv-ed is, *In Re-gi-nen-si a-tri-o:*

REFRAIN

End

Ca-put a-pri de-fe-ro, Red-dens lau-des Do-mi-no.

ANGELS, FROM THE REALMS OF GLORY

Words by James Montgomery

Tune by Henry Smart

1. An - gels, from the realms of glo - ry, Wing your flight o'er all the earth;
2. Shep - herds in the field a - bid - ing, Watch - ing o'er your flocks by night,
3. Sa - ges leave your con - tem - pla - tions; Bright - er vi - sions beam a - far;

Ye, who sang cre - a - tion's sto - ry, Now pro - claim Mes - si - ah's birth:
God with man is now re - sid - ing, Yon - der shines the in - fant light:
Seek the great de - sire of na - tions; Ye have seen his na - tal star:

REFRAIN

Come and wor - ship, come and wor - ship, Wor - ship Christ the new - born King.

4. Saints before the altar bending,
Watching long in hope and fear,
Suddenly the Lord, descending,
In his temple shall appear:
Come and worship, etc.

*5. Though an infant now we view him,
He shall fill his Father's throne,
Gather all the nations to him;
Ev'ry knee shall then bow down:
Come and worship, etc.

*Verse 5 with descant, overleaf

33

Alternative version of verse 5, with
Soprano descant and melody in Alto

5. Though an in - fant now we view him, He shall fill his Fa - ther's throne,

Ga - ther all the na - tions to him; Ev - 'ry knee shall then bow down:

Come and wor - ship, come and wor - ship, Worship Christ the new - born King.

WASSAIL, WASSAIL

English traditional carol

1. Was-sail, was-sail,— all o-ver the—
2. So here is to— Cher-ry and to his right—
3. And here is to— Dob-bin and to his right—

town!—Our—toast it is white, and our ale—it—is brown,
cheek,—Pray—God send our ma-ster a good—piece—of beef,
eye,—Pray—God send our ma-ster a good—Christ-mas pie,

Our—bowl—it—is made of the white—ma-ple
And a good—piece—of—beef—— that— may— we— all—
And a good—Christ-mas—pie—— that— may— we— all—

tree; With the was-sail-ing bowl— we'll—drink— to thee.
see; With the was-sail-ing bowl— we'll—drink— to thee.
see; With the was-sail-ing bowl— we'll—drink— to thee.

4. So|*here is to|Broad May and|to her broad|horn,
   May|God send our|master a|good crop of|corn,
   And a|good crop of|corn that|may we all|see;
   With the|wassailing|bowl we'll|drink to|thee.

5. And|here is to|Fillpail and|to her left|ear,
   Pray|God send our|master a|happy New|Year,
   And a|happy New|Year as|e'er he did|see;
   With our|wassailing|bowl we'll|drink to|thee.

6. And|here is to|Colly and|to her long|tail,
   Pray|God send our|master he|never may|fail
   A|bowl of strong|beer; I|pray you draw|near,
   And|our jolly|wassail it's|then you shall|hear.

7. Come,|butler, come|fill us a|bowl of the|best,
   Then we|hope that your|soul in|heaven may|rest;
   But|if you do|draw us a|bowl of the|small,
   Then|down shall go|butler,|bowl and|all.

8. Then|here's to the|maid in the|lily-white|smock,
   Who|tripped to the|door and|slipped back the|lock!
   Who|tripped to the|door and|pulled back the|pin,
   For to|let these|jolly|wassailers|in.

*Vertical lines indicate bar lines; strong beat follows **bar line.**

COVENTRY CAROL

Fifteenth-century words

Sixteenth-century tune

REFRAIN

End

Lul - ly, lul - la, thou lit - tle ti - ny child, By by, lul - ly lul - lay.

1. O sis - ters too, How may___ we do For to pre - serve this day This___
2. He - rod, the king, In his___ ra - ging, Char-ged he___ hath this day His___
3. That woe is me, Poor child___ for thee! And ev - er___ morn and day, For___

poor___ young - ling, For whom we do___
men___ of might, In his own___
thy___ part - ing Nei - ther say nor___

Repeat REFRAIN only after verse 3.

sing, By by,___ lul - ly lul - lay?
sight, All young chil - dren to slay.
sing By by,___ lul - ly lul - lay!

37

GOD REST YOU MERRY

English traditional carol

1. God rest you merry, gen - tle-men, Let no-thing you dis - may, For Je - sus Christ our
2. From God our heav'n-ly Fa - ther A bless-ed an - gel came, And un - to cer - tain
3. The shep-herds at those ti - dings Re - joic-ed much in mind, And left their flocks a -

Sa - vior Was born up - on this day, To save us
shep - herds Brought ti - dings of the same, How that in
feed - ing, In tem-pest, storm, and wind, And went to

all from Sa - tan's power When we were gone a - stray:
Beth - le - hem was born The son of God by name:
Beth - le - hem straight-way This bless-ed babe to find:

REFRAIN

O____ ti - dings of com - fort and joy, com - fort and joy,___ O____ ti - dings of com - fort and___ joy.

4. But when to Bethlehem they came,
   Whereat this infant lay,
   They found him in a manger,
   Where oxen feed on hay;
   His mother Mary kneeling,
   Unto the Lord did pray:
   O tidings of comfort and joy, etc.

5. Now to the Lord sing praises,
   All you within this place,
   And with true love and brotherhood
   Each other now embrace;
   This holy tide of Christmas
   All others doth deface:
   O tidings of comfort and joy, etc.

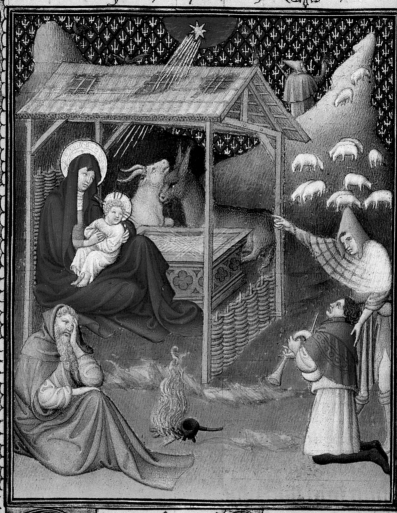

eus m ad   pmine ad adm
utonum   uandum me festina
meum m   loua pu et filio z
tende.   spiritu sancto.

SILENT NIGHT

Tune by Franz Grüber
Words by Joseph Mohr

Si - lent night, ho - ly night,
1. All is calm,___ all is bright___
2. Shep - herds quake___ at the sight;
3. Son of God,___ love's pure light___

Si - lent, ho - ly,

Round yon Vir - gin mo - ther and child, Ho - ly in - fant so ten - der and mild,
Glo - ries stream___ from hea - ven a - far, Heav'n - ly hosts___ sing Al - le - lu - ia;
Ra - diant beams from thy ho___ - ly face, With the dawn of re - deem - ing grace,

Sleep in hea - ven - ly peace,___ Sleep___ in hea - ven - ly peace.
Christ, the Sa - vior, is born,___ Christ,___ the Sa - vior, is born.
Je - sus, Lord, at thy birth,___ Je - sus, Lord, at thy birth.

41

SANS DAY CAROL

Cornish traditional carol

VERSES
1., 2., 3., 4. } Now the hol-ly bears a

ber-ry {
as white as the milk, And__ Ma-ry bore_ Je-sus who was wrapped up in silk:
as green as the grass, And__ Ma-ry bore_ Je-sus who died on the cross:
as black as the coal, And__ Ma-ry bore_ Je-sus who died for us all:
as blood is it red, Then__trust we our__ Sa-vior who rose from the dead:
} And__

REFRAIN

Ma-ry bore_ Je-sus Christ our Sa-vior for to be, And the first tree in the green-wood, it

was_the_hol-ly, hol-ly, hol-ly! And the first tree in the green-wood, it was_the_hol-ly.

42

DECK THE HALL

Welsh traditional carol

1. Deck the hall with boughs of hol - ly,
2. See the blaz - ing yule be - fore us,
3. Fast a - way the old year pass - es,

Fa la la la la, la la la la,

'Tis the sea - son to be jol - ly,
Strike the harp and join the cho - rus,
Hail the new, ye lads and lass - es,

Fa la la la la, la la la la,

44

Don we now our gay ap-pa-rel,
Fol-low me in mer-ry mea-sure, Fa la la, la la la, la la la,
Sing we joy-ous all to-ge-ther,

Don we now our gay ap-pa-rel,
Fol-low me in mer-ry mea-sure, Fa, la la la la la,
Sing we joy-ous all to-ge-ther,

Fa la la la la, la la la la.

Troll the an-cient yule-tide ca-rol,
While I tell of yule-tide trea-sure,
Heed-less of the wind and wea-ther,

Fa la la, la la la la.
Fa la la, la la la la.
Fa la la, la la la la.

Fa la la, la la la la la.

45

JOSEPH DEAREST, JOSEPH MINE

Translated by Neville Stuart Talbot

Fifteenth-century German carol

1. Jo - seph dear - est, Jo - seph mine, Help me cra - dle the child di - vine; God re - ward thee and
2. Glad - ly, dear one, la - dy mine, Help I cra - dle this child of thine; God's own light on us
3. Peace to all that have good-will! God, who hea - ven and earth doth fill, Comes to turn us a -
4. All shall come and bow the knee; Wise and hap - py their souls shall be, Lov - ing such a di -

all___ that's thine In pa - ra - dise, So prays the mo - ther Ma - ry.
both_ shall shine In pa - ra - dise, As prays the mo - ther Ma - ry.
way_ from ill, And lies___ so still With-in the crib of Ma - ry.
vi - ni - ty, As all___ may see In Je - sus, son of Ma - ry.

REFRAIN

He came a - mong us at Christ - mas - tide,___ At Christ - mas - tide,___ In Beth - le - hem; Men shall bring him from far and wide Love's

di - a - dem: Je - sus, Je - sus, Lo, he comes, and loves, and saves, and frees___ us!

47

IN THE BLEAK MIDWINTER

Words by Christina Rossetti

Composed by Gustav Holst

4. Angels and archangels
   May have gathered there,
   Cherubim and seraphim
   Thronged the air:
   But only his mother
   In her maiden bliss
   Worshipped the Beloved
   With a kiss.

5. What can I give him,
   Poor as I am?
   If I were a shepherd
   I would bring a lamb;
   If I were a wise man
   I would do my part;
   Yet what I can I give him,
   Give my heart.

SUSSEX CAROL

English traditional carol

Sop.

1. On Christ-mas night all Christ-ians sing, To hear the news the an-gels bring,
2. Then why should men on earth be so sad, Since our Re-deem-er made us glad,

Sop.
Ah,

Alto
Ah,

Ah,

On Christ-mas night all Christ-ians sing, To hear the news the an-gels bring,
Then why should men on earth be so sad, Since our Re-deem-er made us glad,

Ten.

Bass
Ah,

All

News of great joy, news of great mirth, News of our mer-ci-ful King's birth.
When from our sin he set us free, All for to gain our li-ber-ty?

3. *Sop.:* When sin departs before his grace,
    Then life and health come in its place;
  Ten.: When sin departs before his grace,
    Then life and health come in its place;
  All: Angels and men with joy may sing,
    All for to see the newborn King.

4. *Sop.:* All out of darkness we have light,
    Which made the angels sing this night:
  Ten.: All out of darkness we have light,
    Which made the angels sing this night:
  All: "Glory to God and peace to men,
    Now and forevermore. Amen."

THE HOLLY AND THE IVY

English traditional carol

Solo or small group

1. The hol-ly and the i-vy, When they are both full grown,
2. The hol-ly bears a blos-som As white as the li-ly flower;

All

Of_ all the trees_that are in the wood, The_hol-ly bears the crown.
And_Ma-ry bore_ sweet_ Je-sus Christ To_ be our sweet Sa - vior.

REFRAIN

The ris-ing of the sun,___ The run-ning of the deer,

O, the ris - ing of the sun,___ And the run-ning of the deer,

The_ play-ing of the mer-ry or-gan,___Sweet_sing-ing in the choir.

3. *Solo:* The holly bears a berry
   As red as any blood;
   All: And Mary bore sweet Jesus Christ
   To do poor sinners good.
   O, the rising of the sun, etc.

4. *Solo:* The holly bears a prickle
   As sharp as any thorn;
   All: And Mary bore sweet Jesus Christ
   On Christmas Day in the morn.
   O, the rising of the sun, etc.

5. *Solo:* The holly bears a bark
   As bitter as any gall;
   All: And Mary bore sweet Jesus Christ
   For to redeem us all.
   O, the rising of the sun, etc.

LO, HOW A ROSE

Translated from fifteenth-century German words

Old German tune
harmonized by Michael Praetorius

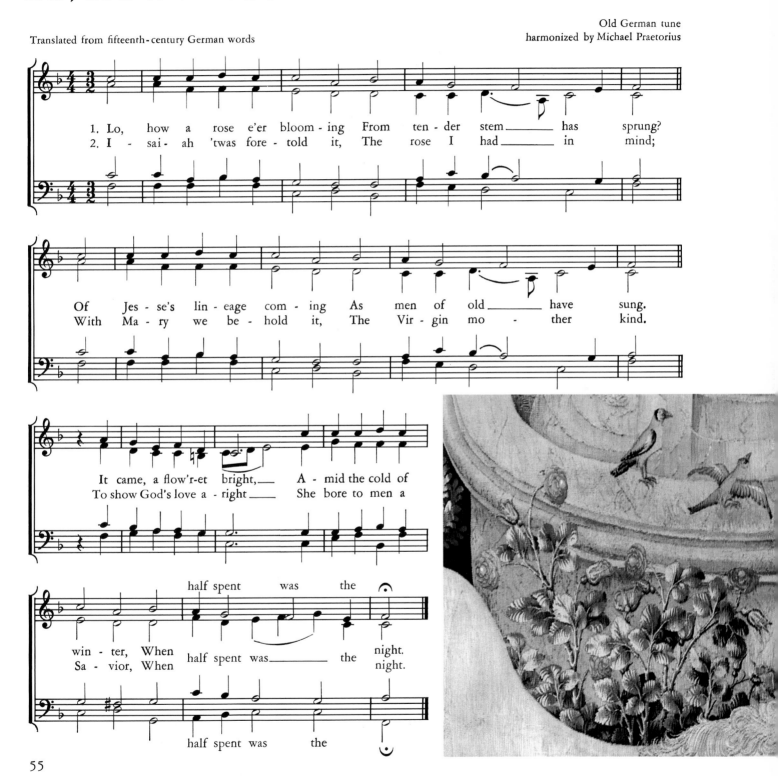

1. Lo, how a rose e'er bloom-ing From ten-der stem____ has sprung?
2. I - sai - ah 'twas fore-told it, The rose I had____ in mind;

Of Jes - se's lin-eage com-ing As men of old____ have sung.
With Ma - ry we be - hold it, The Vir - gin mo - ther kind.

It came, a flow'r-et bright,____ A - mid the cold of
To show God's love a - right____ She bore to men a

half spent was the
win - ter, When half spent was____ the night.
Sa - vior, When night.

half spent was the

JOY TO THE WORLD!

Words by Isaac Watts

Tune by George Frederick Handel
(adapted)

1. Joy to the world!__ the Lord is__come: Let earth re - ceive her
2. Joy to the world!__ the Sa-vior__reigns:Let men their songs em -

King; Let ev - 'ry__ heart_____ pre-pare__ him__ room,_____ And heav'n and na - ture__
ploy, While fields_and__ floods,_____ rocks, hills,__ and__ plains,_____ Re - peat the sound-ing__

Let ev - 'ry heart pre-pare him room, And
While fields and floods, rocks, hills, and plains, Re -

sing, And heav'n and na - ture_ sing, And heav'n,__ and heav'n_and na - ture sing.
joy, Re-peat the sound-ing_ joy, Re - peat,____ re - peat____ the sound-ing joy.

heav'n and na - ture sing, And heav'n and na - ture sing, And heav'n and na - ture_sing.
peat the sound-ing joy, Re - peat the sound-ing joy, Re - peat the sound-ing__ joy.

3. No more let sins and sorrows grow,
   Nor thorns infest the ground;
   He comes to make his blessings flow
   Far as the curse is found.

4. He rules the world with truth and grace,
   And makes the nations prove
   The glories of his righteousness,
   And wonders of his love.

O COME, O COME,

Eighteenth- century words

Fifteenth - century French tune

1. O come, O come, Em - ma - nu - el! Re - deem thy cap - tive

Is - ra - el, That in - to ex - ile drear___ is gone Far

2. O come, thou Branch of Jesse! draw
   The quarry from the lion's claw;
   From the dread caverns of the grave,
   From nether hell, thy people save.
   Rejoice! Rejoice! Emmanuel
   Shall come to thee, O Israel.

3. O come, O come, thou Dayspring bright!
   Pour on our souls thy healing light;
   Dispel the long night's ling'ring gloom,
   And pierce the shadows of the tomb.
   Rejoice! Rejoice! Emmanuel
   Shall come to thee, O Israel.

EMMANUEL

REFRAIN

from the face of God's___ dear son. *Re - joice! Re - joice! Em -*

ma - nu - el Shall come to thee, O Is - ra - el.

4. O come, thou Lord of David's Key!
   The royal door fling wide and free;
   Safeguard for us the heav'nward road,
   And bar the way to death's abode.
   Rejoice! Rejoice! Emmanuel
   Shall come to thee, O Israel.

5. O come, O come, Adonai,
   Who in thy glorious majesty
   From that high mountain clothed with awe
   Gavest thy folk the elder law.
   Rejoice! Rejoice! Emmanuel
   Shall come to thee, O Israel.

INFANT HOLY, INFANT LOWLY

Translated by Edith M. Reed

Polish carol

1. In - fant ho - ly, in - fant low - ly, for his bed a cat - tle stall; Ox - en
2. Flocks were sleep - ing, shep - herds keep - ing vigil till the morn - ing new, Saw the

low - ing lit - tle know - ing Christ the babe is Lord of all. Swift are
glo - ry, heard the sto - ry, ti - dings of a gos - pel true. Thus re -

wing - ing an - gels sing - ing, no - wells ring - ing, ti - dings bring - ing, Christ the
joic - ing, free from sor - row, prais - es voic - ing greet the mor - row, Christ the

babe is Lord of all, Christ the babe is Lord of all.
babe was born for you, Christ the babe was born for you.

61

I SAW THREE SHIPS

English traditional carol

Sop.
1. I saw three ships come sail - ing by,
3. Our Sa - vior Christ and his la - dy,
5. O, they sail'd in - to Beth - le - hem,
7. And all the an - gels in heav'n shall sing,

Alto
Ah,

Ah,

Ten.
Bass

On

I saw three ships come
Our Sa - vior Christ and
O, they sail'd in - to
And all the an - gels in

Christ-mas Day, on Christ-mas Day,

Ah,

Ah,

sail - ing by,
his la - dy,
Beth - le - hem,
heav'n shall sing,

On Christ-mas Day in the morn - ing.

I · SAW · THREE · SHIPS · COME ·
SAILING · BY · COME · SAILING ·
BY

Sop.
Alto
Ah,

2. And what was in those ships all three?
4. Pray, whi - ther sail'd those ships all three?
6. And all the bells on earth shall ring,
8. And all the souls on earth shall sing,

On Christ-mas Day, on Christ-mas Day,

And
Pray,
And
And

Ten.

Bass

Ah,

what was in those ships all three?
whi - ther sail'd those ships all three?
all the bells on earth shall ring,
all the souls on earth shall sing,

On Christ-mas Day in the morn - ing.

9. Then let us all re - joice a - main! *On Christ - mas Day, on Christ - mas Day,* Then

let us all re - joice a - main! *On Christ - mas Day in the morn - ing.*

ONCE IN ROYAL DAVID'S CITY

Words by Cecil Frances Alexander

Tune by Henry J. Gauntlett

1. Once in roy-al David's ci-ty Stood a low-ly cat-tle shed,
2. He came down to earth from hea-ven Who is God and Lord of all,
3. And through all his won-drous child-hood He would ho-nor and o-bey,

Where a mo-ther laid her ba-by In a man-ger for his bed;
And his shel-ter was a sta-ble, And his cra-dle was a stall;
Love and watch the low-ly maid-en, In whose gen-tle arms he lay;

Ma-ry was that mo-ther mild, Je-sus Christ her lit-tle child.
With the poor and mean and low-ly, Lived on earth our Sa-vior ho-ly.
Chris-tian chil-dren all must be Mild, o-be-dient, good as he.

4. For he is our childhood's pattern,
Day by day like us he grew,
He was little, weak and helpless,
Tears and smiles like us he knew;
And he feeleth for our sadness,
And he shareth in our gladness.

5. And our eyes at last shall see him,
Through his own redeeming love,
For that child so dear and gentle
Is our Lord in heaven above;
And he leads his children on
To the place where he is gone.

6. Not in that poor lowly stable,
With the oxen standing by,
We shall see him; but in heaven,
Set at God's right hand on high;
Where like stars his children crowned
All in white shall wait around.

O COME, ALL YE FAITHFUL

Tune by John Francis Wade
Translated by Frederick Oakeley and William Thomas Brooke

Descant for verse 3 for Soprano solo or small group

3. Sing, choirs of an - gels, Sing, sing in ex - ul - ta - tion, all ye

1. O come, all ye faith - ful, Joy - ful and tri - um - phant, O
2. God of God, Light of light,
3. Sing, choirs of an - gels, Sing in ex - ul - ta - tion,
4. Yea, Lord, we greet thee, Born this hap - py morn - ing,

ci - ti - zens of heav'n, all ye ci - ti - zens of heav'n, of heav'n a - bove; Sing, sing,

come ye, O come ye to Beth - le - hem;
Lo! he ab - hors not the Vir - gin's womb;
Sing, all ye ci - ti - zens of heav'n a - bove;
Je - sus, to thee be glo - ry giv'n;

glo - ry to God, to God in the high - est: O

REFRAIN

Come and be - hold him, Born the King of an - gels:
Ve - ry God, Be - got - ten not cre - a - ted:
Glo - ry to God In the high - est:
Word of the Fa - ther, Now in flesh ap - pear - ing:

O come, let us a -

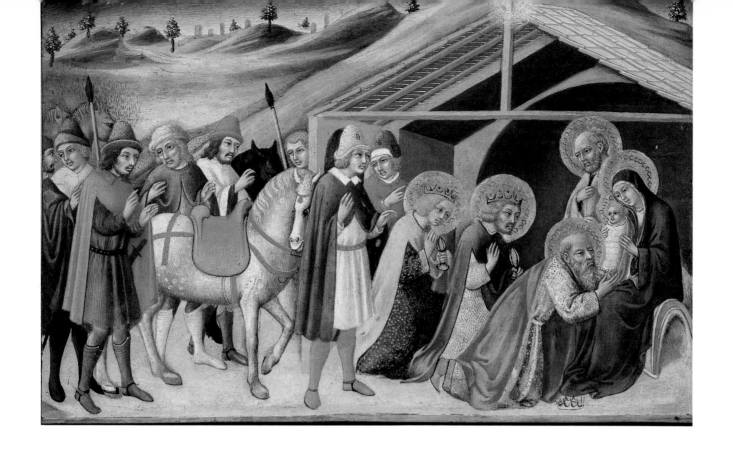

come, let us a - dore him, O come, let us a - dore him,

dore him, O come, let us a - dore him, O

O come, let us a - dore him, a - dore him, Christ the Lord.

come, let us a - dore him, Christ the Lord.

THE THREE KINGS

Translated by H. N. Bate

Tune by Peter Cornelius
(adapted)

Solo or small group

1. Three kings from Per - sian lands a - far To Jor-dan fol-low the

How bright - ly shines the

point-ing star: And this the quest of the tra - vel-ers three, Where the new-born King of the Jews may— be.

morn - ing star! With grace and truth from heav'n— a -

Full roy - al gifts they bear for the King; Gold, in - cense,— myrrh— are their of - fer - ing.

far Our Jes - se tree— now— blow -

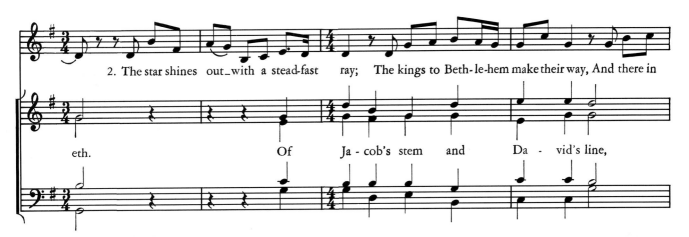

2. The star shines out with a stead-fast ray; The kings to Beth-le-hem make their way, And there in

eth. Of Ja - cob's stem and Da - vid's line,

wor-ship they bend the knee, As Ma-ry's child in her lap they see; Their roy-al gifts they show to the

For thee, my bride-groom, King di-vine, My

King: Gold, in-cense, myrrh are their of-fer-ing. 3. Thou child of man, lo, to Beth-le-hem

soul with love o'er-flow-eth. Thy word, thy word,

The kings are tra-v'ling, tra-vel with them! The star of mer-cy, the star of grace, Shall lead thy heart to its rest-ing

Je-su, Je-su, In-ly feeds us, Right-ly leads us,

70

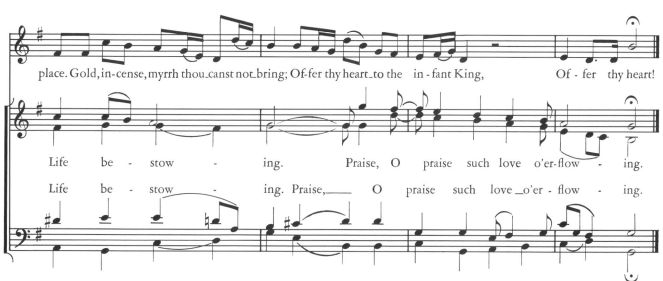

place. Gold, in-cense, myrrh thou canst not bring; Of-fer thy heart to the in-fant King, Of-fer thy heart!

Life be-stow - ing. Praise, O praise such love o'er-flow - ing.

Life be-stow - ing. Praise, O praise such love o'er-flow - ing.

CHRISTMAS EVE

HERE WE COME A-WASSAILING

English traditional carol

1. Here we come a-was-sail-ing A-mong the leaves so green,
2. Our was-sail cup is made___ of The rose-ma-ry tree,

Here we come a-wan-der-ing, So fair___ to be seen:
And so is your beer Of the best___ bar-ley:

72

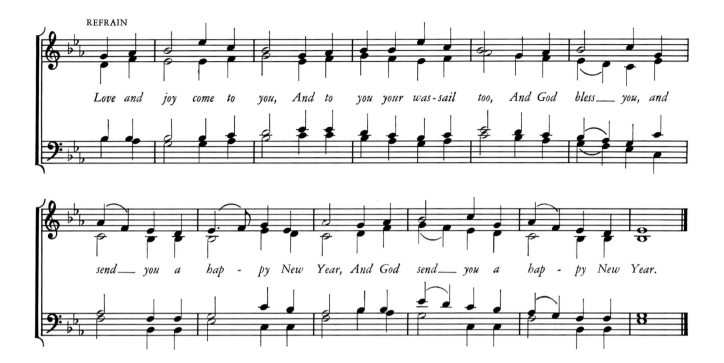

REFRAIN

Love and joy come to you, And to you your was-sail too, And God bless___ you, and

send___ you a hap-py New Year, And God send___ you a hap-py New Year.

3. We |*are not daily| beggars
That| beg from door to| door,
But| we are neighbors'| children
Whom| you have seen be|fore:
Love and joy come to you, etc.

4. Call| up the butler | of this house,
Put| on his golden| ring;
Let him| bring us up a| glass of beer,
And| better shall we| sing:
Love and joy come to you, etc.

5. We've| got a little| purse
Of | stretching leather| skin;
We| want a little of| your money
To| line it well with| in:
Love and joy come to you, etc.

6. | Bring us out a | table,
And| spread it with a| cloth;
| Bring us out a| moldy cheese,
And| some of your Christmas| loaf:
Love and joy come to you, etc.

7. God| bless the master| of this house,
Like| wise the mistress | too;
And | all the little| children
That| round the table | go:
Love and joy come to you, etc.

8. Good| Master and good| Mistress,
While you're| sitting by the | fire,
Pray| think of us poor| children
That's| wandered in the| mire:
Love and joy come to you, etc.

* Vertical lines indicate bar lines;
  strong beat follows bar line.

ROCKING

Translated by Percy Dearmer

Czech carol

1. Lit - tle Je - sus, sweet - ly sleep, do not stir; We will lend a coat of fur,
2. Ma - ry's lit - tle ba - by, sleep, sweet - ly sleep, Sleep in com - fort, slum - ber deep;

We will rock you, rock you, rock you, We will rock you, rock you, rock you:

See the fur to keep you warm, Snug - ly round your ti - ny form.
We will serve you all we can, Dar - ling, dar - ling lit - tle man.

74

WHILE SHEPHERDS WATCHED THEIR FLOCKS

Words by Nahum Tate

Tune from *Este's Psalter*, sixteenth century

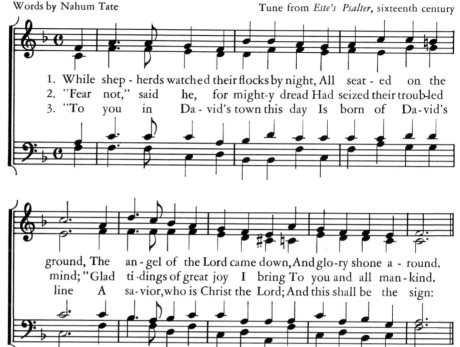

1. While shep-herds watched their flocks by night, All seat-ed on the
2. "Fear not," said he, for might-y dread Had seized their troub-led
3. "To you in Da-vid's town this day Is born of Da-vid's

ground, The an-gel of the Lord came down, And glo-ry shone a-round.
mind; "Glad ti-dings of great joy I bring To you and all man-kind.
line A sa-vior, who is Christ the Lord; And this shall be the sign:

Alternative version of verse 6, with Soprano descant and melody in Alto

6. "All glo-ry be to God on high, And on the earth be peace; Good-

will hence-forth from heav'n to men Be-gin and ne-ver cease."

4. "The heav'nly babe you there
      shall find
   To human view displayed,
   All meanly wrapped in swathing
      bands,
   And in a manger laid."

5. Thus spake the seraph, and
      forthwith
   Appeared a shining throng
   Of angels praising God, who thus
   Addressed their joyful song:

6. "All glory be to God on high,
   And on the earth be peace;
   Goodwill henceforth from
      heav'n to men
   Begin and never cease."

eus mad   omine ad adui

autorium   uandum me festina.

meum in   loria pri et filio

tende.   et spiritu sancto.

WE THREE KINGS OF ORIENT ARE

Words and tune by John Henry Hopkins

1. We three kings of O - ri - ent are; Bear - ing gifts we tra - verse a - far

Field and foun - tain, moor and moun - tain, Fol - low - ing yon - der star:

REFRAIN

O_____ star of won - der, star of night, Star with roy - al beau - ty bright,

West - ward lead - ing, still pro - ceed - ing, Guide us to thy per - fect light.

Melchior:

2. Born a king on Bethlehem plain,
   Gold I bring, to crown him again,
   King forever, ceasing never,
   Over us all to reign:
   O star of wonder, etc.

Caspar:

3. Frankincense to offer have I,
   Incense owns a deity nigh;
   Prayer and praising, all men raising,
   Worship him, God most high:
   O star of wonder, etc.

Balthazar:

4. Myrrh is mine; its bitter perfume
   Breathes a life of gathering gloom;
   Sorrowing, sighing, bleeding, dying,
   Sealed in the stone-cold tomb:
   O star of wonder, etc.

All:

5. Glorious now behold him arise,
   King and God and sacrifice,
   Alleluia, alleluia,
   Earth to the heav'ns replies:
   O star of wonder, etc.

PATAPAN

Translated by Percy Dearmer

Burgundian tune

1. Wil - lie, take your lit - tle drum, With your whis - tle,
2. Thus the men of old - en days Loved the King of
3. God and man are now be - come More at one than

Prom, pom, pom,   *Prom, pom, pom,*

Prom, pom, pom,

Ro - bin come! When we hear the fife and drum,
Kings to praise: When they hear the fife and drum,
fife and drum. When you hear the fife and drum,

Tu-re-lu-re-lu, pat-a-pat-a-pan,

When we
When they
When you

Prom, pom, pom,   *Prom, pom, pom,*   *Prom, pom, pom,*

80

hear the fife and drum, Christ-mas should be__ fro - lic - some.
hear the fife and drum, Sure our chil - dren__ won't be dumb!
hear the fife and drum, Dance, and make the__ vil - lage hum.

Prom, pom, pom, pom, pom, pom, pom, pom. Prom, pom, pom.

WHENCE COMES THIS RUSH OF WINGS?

French traditional carol

1. Whence comes this rush of wings a - far,
2. "Tell us, ye birds, why come ye here,
3. An - gels and shep - herds, birds of the sky,

Fol - low - ing straight the No - well star?
In - to this sta - ble, poor and drear?"
Come where the son of God doth lie;

Birds from the woods in won - drous flight,
"Has - t'ning we seek the new - born King,
Christ on earth with man doth dwell,

Beth - le - hem seek this ho - ly night.
And all our sweet - est mu - sic bring."
Join in the shout "No - well, No - well!"

83

THE TWELVE DAYS

English traditional carol

VERSES 1–4

1. On the first* day of Christ-mas my
2. On the se-cond* day of Christ-mas my

true love sent to me a
true love sent to me

four call-ing birds, three French hens, two tur-tle doves,
four three two
and a par-tridge in a pear tree.

VERSES 5–12

5. On the fifth* day of Christ-mas my true love sent to me
6. On the sixth* day of Christ-mas my true love sent to me
twelve drum-mers drum-ming,
twelve

*Sing appropriate number of day, and then cut from † to appropriate boxed number.

84

OF CHRISTMAS

e-lev'n pi-pers pi-ping, ten lords a-leap-ing,
e-lev'n   ten

nine la-dies danc-ing, eight maids a-milk-ing,
nine   eight

sev'n swans a-swim-ming, six geese a-lay-ing, five gold rings, four___ call-ing birds,
sev'n   six

three French hens, two___ tur-tle doves, and a par-tridge___ in a pear tree.

WHAT CHILD IS THIS?

Words by William Chatterton Dix

English traditional tune

1. What child is this, who, laid to rest,__ On Ma-ry's lap__ is sleep-ing?__ Whom
2. Why lies he in__ such mean es-tate,__ Where ox and ass__ are feed-ing?__ Good
3. So bring him in-cense, gold and myrrh;__ Come, pea-sant, king,__ to own__ him._ The

an-gels greet__ with an-thems sweet,__ While shep-herds watch__ are keep-ing?
Chris-tian, fear, for sin-ners here__ The si-lent Word__ is plead-ing.
King of Kings__ sal-va-tion brings;__ Let lov-ing hearts__ en-throne him.

This,__ this__ is Christ__ the King,__ Whom shep-herds guard__ and an-gels sing!__
Nails,__ spear__ shall pierce__ him through,__ The cross be borne__ for me, for you.__
Raise,__ raise__ the song__ on high!__ The Vir-gin sings__ her lul-la-by.

Haste,__ haste__ to bring__ him laud,__ The babe,__ the son__ of Ma-ry!
Hail,__ hail,__ the Word__ made flesh,__ The babe,__ the son__ of Ma-ry!
Joy,__ joy,__ for Christ__ is born,__ The babe,__ the son__ of Ma-ry!

O CHRISTMAS TREE

Words by E. G. Anschütz

German folk song

1. O Christ-mas tree, O Christ-mas tree! Thou tree most fair and love-ly!
2. O Christ-mas tree, O Christ-mas tree! Thou hast a won-drous mes-sage.

O Christ-mas tree, O Christ-mas tree, Thou tree most fair and love-ly!
O Christ-mas tree, O Christ-mas tree, Thou hast a won-drous mes-sage.

The sight of thee at Christ-mas-tide Spreads hope and glad-ness far and wide.
Thou dost pro-claim the Sa-vior's birth, Good-will to men and peace on earth.

O Christ-mas tree, O Christ-mas tree! Thou tree most fair and love-ly!
O Christ-mas tree, O Christ-mas tree! Thou hast a won-drous mes-sage.

DING DONG! MERRILY ON HIGH

Sixteenth-century French tune
Words by George R. Woodward

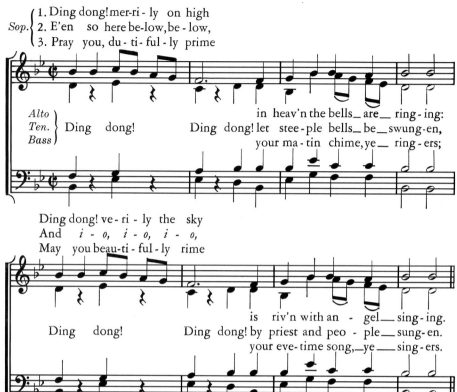

Sop.
1. Ding dong! mer-ri - ly on high
2. E'en so here be-low, be - low,
3. Pray you, du - ti - ful - ly prime

Alto
Ten.
Bass
Ding dong!
in heav'n the bells___ are___ ring - ing:
Ding dong! let stee-ple bells___ be___ swung-en,
your ma - tin chime, ye___ ring - ers;

Ding dong! ve - ri - ly the sky
And i - o, i - o, i - o,
May you beau-ti - ful - ly rime

Ding dong!
is riv'n with an - gel___ sing - ing.
Ding dong! by priest and peo - ple___ sung-en.
your eve - time song, ye___ sing - ers.

REFRAIN

Glo

- - - ri - a, Ho - san - na in ex - cel - sis!

i-o pronounced ee-o

90

WE WISH YOU A MERRY CHRISTMAS

West-of-England traditional carol

1. We wish you a mer-ry Christ-mas, We wish you a mer-ry Christ-mas, We
2. Now bring us some fig-gy pud-ding, Now bring us some fig-gy pud-ding, Now
3. For we all like fig-gy pud-ding, We all like fig-gy pud-ding, We

wish you a mer-ry Christ-mas And a hap-py New Year.
bring us some fig-gy pud-ding, And bring some out here.
all like fig-gy pud-ding, So bring some out here.

REFRAIN

Good ti-dings we bring to you and your kin; We

wish you a mer-ry Christ-mas and a hap-py New Year.

4. And we won't go till we've got some,
   We won't go till we've got some,
   We won't go till we've got some,
   So bring some out here.
   Good tidings we bring, etc.

ACKNOWLEDGMENTS

Page 12, "O Little Town of Bethlehem" (British edition only): music ("Forest Green") collected and arranged by Ralph Vaughan Williams (1872-1958), adapted by David Willcocks, by special permission of Oxford University Press

Page 29, "Bring a Torch, Jeannette, Isabella:" words by permission of the publisher, The Boston Music Company, Boston, MA 02116

Page 35, "Wassail, Wassail:" melody collected by Ralph Vaughan Williams (1872-1958), by permission of Oxford University Press

Page 48, "In the Bleak Midwinter:" tune ("Cranham") by Gustav Holst (1874-1934) from the *English Hymnal,* by permission of Oxford University Press

Page 50, "Sussex Carol:" melody and words collected by Ralph Vaughan Williams (1872-1958), by permission of Mrs. Ralph Vaughan Williams and Oxford University Press

Page 61, "Infant Holy, Infant Lowly:" words from *The Kingsway Carol Book,* edited by Leslie Russell, by permission of Bell & Hyman Ltd., London

Page 90, "Ding Dong! Merrily on High:" words by G. R. Woodward reproduced by permission of SPCK

The following are reproduced from *The Oxford Book of Carols* by permission of Oxford University Press:

Page 27, "O Little One Sweet:" translation by Percy Dearmer
Page 42, "Sans Day Carol:" words collated by Percy Dearmer
Page 47, "Joseph Dearest, Joseph Mine:" translation by Neville Stuart Talbot
Page 68, "The Three Kings:" translation by H. N. Bate
Page 74, "Rocking:" Czech melody collected by Martin Shaw; translation by Percy Dearmer
Page 80, "Patapan:" translation by Percy Dearmer

LIST OF ILLUSTRATIONS

The works of art in this book, with four exceptions, were photographed by The Metropolitan Museum of Art Photograph Studio; the photographs on pages 37, 40, and 77 were taken by Charles Passela and are provided courtesy of George Braziller, Inc.; the photograph on page 76 was taken by Timothy Husband.

Pages 30-31: *The Story of Esther*
Marco del Buono Giamberti, Italian
(Florentine), 1402-1489
Apollonio di Giovanni di Tomaso, Italian
(Florentine), 1415/17-1465
Cassone panel, tempera and gold on wood

Rogers Fund, 1918   18.117.2

Page 32: *The Nativity* (detail)
Gerard David, Flemish, active ca. 1484,
d. 1523
Central panel of a triptych, tempera and oil on
canvas

The Jules Bache Collection, 1949   49.7.20b

Page 34: *Censing Angels*
Stained-glass panel (detail)
Cathedral of Saint-Pierre, Troyes
French, ca. 1170-80

Gift of Ella Brummer, in memory of her late husband,
Ernest Brummer, 1977   77.346.1

Page 35: Woodcut from *Crawhall's Chap-Book
Chaplets,* London, 1883
Joseph Crawhall, British, 1860-1916

Harris Brisbane Dick Fund   840 ref

Page 36: *Rest on the Flight into Egypt*
Gerard David, Flemish, active ca. 1484,
d. 1523
Tempera and oil on wood

The Jules Bache Collection, 1949   49.7.21

Page 37: *Flight into Egypt*
Illuminated manuscript page (detail) from the
Belles Heures of Jean, Duke of Berry
Pol, Jean, and Herman de Limbourg, French
(Paris), active ca. 1400-16
Tempera and gold on vellum

The Cloisters Collection, 1954   54.1.1

Page 39: *Paradise*
Giovanni di Paolo, Italian (Sienese),
1403(?)-1482/83
Tempera and gold on canvas

Rogers Fund, 1906   06.1046

Page 40: *The Nativity*
Illuminated manuscript page from the *Belles
Heures* of Jean, Duke of Berry
Pol, Jean, and Herman de Limbourg, French
(Paris), active ca. 1400-16
Tempera and gold on vellum

The Cloisters Collection, 1954   54.1.1

Page 41: *Angel*
Figure from a carved oak choir stall
French, second half 15th century

Gift of J. Pierpont Morgan, 1917   17.190.378

Pages 42, 43: *Virgin and Child with Angels*
(detail and full image)
Bernaert van Orley, Flemish, ca.
1492-1541/42
Tempera and oil on wood

Bequest of Benjamin Altman, 1913   14.40.632

Pages 44-45: *Marriage Feast at Cana*
Anders Pålsson, Swedish, 1781-1849
Painted linen wall hanging (detail)

Gift of Mr. and Mrs. William Maxwell Evarts, 1953
53.98

Page 46: *Miracle of the Palm Tree*
Polychromed and gilded walnut relief
North Spanish, ca. 1490-1510

Rogers Fund, 1938   38.184

Page 49: *The Nativity*
Workshop of Fra Angelico, Italian
(Florentine), 1387-1455
Tempera on wood

Rogers Fund, 1924   24.22

Page 50: *Madonna and Child with Angels*
(details)
Pietro di Domenico da Montepulciano, Italian
(Marchigian), active early 15th century
Tempera on wood, gold ground, 1420

Roger Fund, 1907   07.201

Page 51: *The Annunciation*
Robert Campin, Flemish, active by 1406,
d. 1444
Central panel of *The Campin Altarpiece,*
triptych, oil on wood, ca. 1425

The Cloisters Collection, 1956   56.70

Page 52: *The Unicorn Leaps the Stream* (detail)
Tapestry in the series *The Hunt of the Unicorn*
Silk, wool, and metal thread
French or Flemish, ca. 1500

Gift of John D. Rockefeller, Jr., 1937   37.80.3

Page 53: Needlework back of a Queen Anne
easy chair (detail)
Crewel on canvas
American (Newport, Rhode Island), 1758

Gift of Mrs. J. Insley Blair, 1950   50.228.3

Page 54: *Madonna and Child*
Donato de' Bardi, Italian (Lombard), active by
1426, d. 1450/51
Central panel of a triptych; tempera on wood,
gold ground

Gift of Samuel H. Kress Foundation, 1937   37.163.2

Page 55: *The Unicorn Dips His Horn into the
Stream* (detail)
Tapestry in the series *The Hunt of the Unicorn*
Silk, wool, and metal thread
French or Flemish, ca. 1500

Gift of John D. Rockefeller, Jr., 1937   37.80.2

Pages 56, 57: *Retable of Le Cellier* (details)
Jean Bellegambe, French, ca. 1467/77-1535
Central panel of a triptych, tempera and oil on
wood

Bequest of Michael Friedsam, 1931, The Friedsam
Collection   32.100.102

Pages 58, 59: *Adoration of the Magi* and *Flight
into Egypt*
Adriaen Isenbrant, Flemish, active by 1510,
d. 1551
Left and right panels of a triptych, tempera
and oil on wood

Frederick C. Hewitt Fund, 1913   13.32a, c

Page 60: Illuminated manuscript page
(detail)
Tempera and gold leaf on parchment
Italian (North Central), 15th century

Gift of Louis L. Lorillard, 1896   272.1 L48f

Page 61: *The Virgin with the Child
in Swaddling Clothes*
Albrecht Dürer, German, 1471-1528
Woodcut

Harris Brisbane Dick Fund, 1931   31.57.2

Page 62: Illustration for "I Saw Three Ships,"
from *A Book of Nursery Rhymes,* New York,
1897
Francis D. Bedford, British, 1864-1934

The Elisha Whittelsey Collection, The Elisha Whittelsey
Fund, 1966   66.540.2

Page 64: *The Nativity*
Adriaen Isenbrant, Flemish, active by 1510,
d. 1551
Central panel of a triptych, tempera and oil on
wood

Frederick C. Hewitt Fund, 1913   13.32b

94

Page 67: *Adoration of the Magi*
Sano di Pietro, Italian (Sienese), 1406-1481
Tempera and gold on wood

Gift of Irma N. Straus, 1958   58.189.2

Page 68: *The Nativity* (detail)
Stained-glass panel
Carmelite Church, Boppard-on-the-Rhine
German, 1445

Francis L. Leland Fund, 1913   13.64.4

Page 69: *The Three Magi*
Attributed to the Master of Ottobeuren,
    German
Wood, gesso, polychrome, and gilding,
    ca. 1515-20

Purchase, Joseph Pulitzer Bequest, 1951   51.28

Page 71: Chasuble (detail)
Red velvet embroidered in gold thread,
    decorated with seed pearls
English, first third 14th century

Fletcher Fund, 1927   27.162.1

Pages 72, 73: Illustrations from *Gleanings
    from the "Graphic,"* London, 1889
Randolph Caldecott, British, 1846-1886

Gift of Juliet W. Robinson, 1918   18.77

Page 74: *Crib of the Infant Jesus*
Carved and polychromed oak, lead, silver gilt,
    painted parchment, and silk embroidered
    with seed pearls and translucent enamels
South Netherlandish (Brabant), 15th century

Gift of Ruth Blumka, as a memorial to her late husband's
ideals, 1974   1974.121

Page 75: *The Nativity*
Stained-glass panel
Carmelite Church, Boppard-on-the-Rhine
German, 1445

Francis L. Leland Fund, 1913   13.64.4

Page 76: *Angel Playing a Rebec*
Painted and gilded wood, German, ca. 1500

Gift of Abby Aldrich Rockefeller, 1947   47.89.2

Page 77: *Annunciation to the Shepherds*
Illuminated manuscript page from the *Belles
    Heures* of Jean, Duke of Berry
Pol, Jean, and Herman de Limbourg, French
    (Paris), active ca. 1400-16
Tempera and gold on vellum

The Cloisters Collection, 1954   54.1.1

Page 79: *Journey of the Magi*
Sassetta (Stefano di Giovanni), Italian
    (Sienese), ca. 1392-1450/51
Tempera on wood

Bequest of Maitland F. Griggs, 1943, Maitland F. Griggs
Collection   43.98.1

Page 80: *Retable of Le Cellier* (details)
Jean Bellegambe, French, ca. 1467/77-1535
Left and right panels of a triptych, tempera
    and oil on wood

Bequest of Michael Friedsam, 1931, The Friedsam
Collection   32.100.102

Page 81: Illustration from a tournament
    manuscript
Ink and watercolor with gold
German (Nuremberg), late 16th century

Rogers Fund, 1922   959.4 T64

Page 82: Postcard
Franz Karl Delavilla, Austrian, 1884-1967
Color linocut published by the Wiener
    Werkstätte, Vienna, ca. 1910

Museum Accession, 1943

Page 83: Stained-glass quatrefoil
Austrian (Ebreichsdorf, near Wiener
    Neustadt), ca. 1380

The Cloisters Collection, 1936   36.39.2

Page 84: Embroidered picture (detail)
Silk, metal thread, and purl on silk
English, third quarter 17th century

Bequest of Carolyn L. Griggs, 1950   50.204.2

Page 85: Album quilt (detail)
Cotton appliqué
American (Baltimore, Maryland), ca. 1850

Sansbury-Mills Fund, 1974   74.24

Page 87: *Madonna and Child*
Andrea della Robbia, Italian (Florentine),
    1435-1525
Glazed terra-cotta relief

Gift of Edith and Herbert Lehman Foundation, Inc.,
1969   69.113

Page 88: Crèche (detail)
Figures of polychromed terra cotta and wood,
    with silk robes
Italian (Neapolitan), 18th century

Gift of Loretta Hines Howard, 1964   64.164.1-167

Page 90: Postcard
Valerie Petter, Austrian, 1881-1963
Color linocut published by the Wiener
    Werkstätte, Vienna, ca. 1910

Museum Accession, 1943

Page 91: Cover design for *St. Nicholas*
    magazine
Will Bradley, American, 1868-1962

Gift of Mrs. Fern Bradley Dufner, 1952   52.625.104

INDEX OF FIRST LINES